ESPRESSO
YOURSELF

The Taste Of Your Brand

. . . .

ANGI EGAN

ESPRESSO YOURSELF

Espresso Yourself – The Taste Of Your Brand.
© Angi Egan.

ISBN: 978-1-906316-32-7.

All rights reserved.

Published in 2009 by Word4Word, Evesham, UK.
www.w4wdp.com

The right of Angi Egan to be identified as the author of
this work has been asserted by her in accordance with the
Copyright, Designs and Patents Act 1988.

A CIP record of this book is available from the British Library.

No part of this publication may be reproduced in any form or
by any means without permission from the author.

Printed in the UK by TJ International, Padstow.

Liz,

We speak the same language — you just do it in a far sexier accent! :)

Keep shining.

Angi

Preface

Preface

I have always maintained that playing things safe leads to becoming a 'me too brand'. This is a dangerous strategy when planning for the long-term commercial success of any business. Sadly, it seems when the economic climate is a challenging one this is the position many businesses take.

This inevitably leads to a loss of focus for you, your team and, more dangerously, your customers. Your focus becomes consumed with what everyone else is doing so that you don't fall out of step. It also means you're falling into copying the competition.

Dare to be different. Be remarkable. Have the courage to be authentically you.

Having learnt from some of the most sustained brand successes of the past 20 years, I can see that they have maintained a laser-like focus on the simple principles of brand longevity – buy for the customer, remain disciplined and focused, keep control and avoid corporate thinking.

This demands a return to 'old fashioned' thinking that creates a renaissance in service excellence. Put simply, this is operating at every level to serve the customer. Be this the team who represent your brand, or the paying punter. It means moving away from a culture shaped by 'the computer says no' to a more empowered and flexible 'how can we make that happen' mentality.

I remain consistently despondent with the service encountered in the UK – a one where I'm either comprehensively ignored or one where I'm met with intransigent, unimaginative automatons hemmed in by corporate thinking and restrictive company policies.

We must embrace entirely the notion that every encounter counts. A determination to truly demonstrate our service excellence by ensuring our customers leave richer for the experience and inspired by our knowledge. This requires energetic maintenance by everyone involved in order to deliver sustained results.

The time has come for us to quit offering excuses and reasons and instead focus on results.

If we truly want to romance our customers then constant effort is required. The alternative is promiscuity, wanderlust and costly break-ups...

    Angi Egan

······
Dedication

Dedication

To Mick & the hairy blonde – proof that romance is alive & kicking – thank you 'man of the world' x

Dobbsie baby – there is no end to your talents… business mentor, confidant, friend, arse kicker and now editor! Thank you for everything, you'll simply never, ever know.

TP – learning to open the door, and letting it go…

John Wilson – for your brilliance at providing the kiss and sell paragraph on page 24. Sublime, astute and germane. Totally you. Deep thanks and appreciation.

Contents

	Introduction	13
CHAPTER ONE:	Interrupt the pattern	17
CHAPTER TWO:	Dare to be different	27
CHAPTER THREE:	The power of a good word	37
CHAPTER FOUR:	The power of a good spoken word	43
CHAPTER FIVE:	What do people really say?	49
CHAPTER SIX:	Get away from the given!	55
CHAPTER SEVEN:	It's not about you!	63
CHAPTER EIGHT:	Wake me up or I'll go go	69
CHAPTER NINE:	Craft a top 5	73
CHAPTER TEN:	Conclusion	85
	About the author	89
	What people say about Angi Egan	93

......

Introduction

Introduction

Espresso Yourself is the second in the series of *Romancing the Customer™* business guides – a slightly mischievous, innovative and significant observation of what makes iconic businesses stand out, prosper and leave their customers longing for more.

It will provide a brief introduction to the thinking of *Romancing the Customer™* and why you need to consider the five senses as part of your plan for brand communication and successful sales. *Romancing the Customer™* draws on the many parallels that exist between great relationships and great businesses. The aim for both is unquestionably to create loyalty, pleasure and longevity of relationships which avoid the pitfalls of boredom, indifference and promiscuity.

Initial Lust was the first in the series and focuses on the simple steps you can take that are a joy to implement but do not cost a fortune. Most of all, they ensure your business stands out from

the competition in a saturated market place.
Initial Lust also contains the key principles to visual communication and brand marketing. Many brands unwittingly damage or totally destroy their customers' trust and confidence through visual mumbling and clumsy fumbling.

Espresso Yourself is concerned with the taste of your brand – the 'how do customers really feel about what I do?' This has little to do with whether they think you're a jolly good egg, or even that you're competent at what you do. *Espresso Yourself* is all about the actions you, and those who represent your brand, take on a consistent basis to enrich and intensify the feelings you have evoked in the mind of your customer (assuming you have evoked the ones you were aiming for in the first place, otherwise it will all end in tears).

Since writing and speaking about the principles of *Romancing the Customer*™ (an ideal job for a woman – getting paid to talk!), I have received great feedback and many comments, the most frequent of which is: "This is just common sense Angi".

INTRODUCTION

I agree – it is all obvious stuff. The message of service excellence isn't something I invented, and the idea that we have to create products and services that customers are going to love is not exactly rocket science.

What I say in response is: "Common sense is rarely common practice."

In many ways the simple message from the *Romancing the Customer*™ series acts as a reminder of something you used to do but somehow stopped doing. Just like in the world of relationships really. Business and the world of romance have so much in common and, through this series of business guides, I'll share some of these parallels. It may well offer you a fresh perspective on an old subject, or if I'm really fortunate it will teach you something you hadn't even thought of.

Read on to discover what you can do to create feelings of brand love (fidelity) and strengthen your brand authority…

CHAPTER ONE

......

Interrupt the pattern

Interrupt the pattern

Espresso Yourself is about the taste of your brand and interrupting patterns of behaviour many of our customers fall into. This is what I describe as default coma mode – where customers are running on auto pilot and able to predict what you're going to say or do next. This is frustrating at best and leads to indifference and cynicism at worst.

Now, more than ever, there must be a renaissance in great service, inspired expertise and creative thinking by businesses. Great service alone would be sufficient to break a customer's reverie or awake them from their coma.

Think about yourself as a customer. When was the last time someone served you so brilliantly they really woke you up? Interrupting the pattern is about doing things differently from everyone else. It involves looking at the areas in your business where predictability lurks: perhaps the visual cliché we looked at in *Initial Lust* or the voicemail that does little to describe what you can do for me.

There is a fine balance between meeting expectations and being dull and predictable. The brands and organisations that thrive and prosper are those who consistently think and behave differently, yet in a way that enforces their values and continually engages their customers rather than alienates them. Especially when the economic climate means we're faced with extra challenges.

Inspiration to take continued action is the key to business success. As I've already mentioned, the principles in the *Romancing the Customer*™ series are those that have stood the test of time. They have been written and talked about and possibly even reinvented on countless occasions.

So why, oh why, do we continue to encounter poor service, sloppy standards and huge indifference from businesses in the UK (many of whom are the first to wring their hands in despair while claiming they've tried everything and nothing works)?

INTERRUPT THE PATTERN

Please indulge me for a moment while I share a story to illustrate my point. It's about an old man out walking his dog. A young woman approaches the old man with her young pups and, like all dog owners, the conversation centres on the respective merits of their pets. She listens intently and is mightily impressed by the stories the old man shares about the amazing tricks his dog knows. After listening in wonderment, and tempted to admonish her young pups, the young woman eventually asks if the old man would get his dog to show her one of his tricks. Astonished, and slightly amused by the young woman's request, the old man chuckles and replies: "Oh, he doesn't do the tricks, he just *knows* the tricks."

> *"Success is not the key to happiness, but happiness is the key to success.*
> *If you love what you are doing you will become successful"* Benjamin Disraeli

ESPRESSO YOURSELF

And so it is in business. We all talk about the principles. We all know what the principles are. Yet seldom is sustained action taken to put them into practice.

The pattern that exists in the UK service industry is one of indifference, boredom and poor awareness from the people employed to serve us. If we are to survive as a service economy then continued steps must be taken to interrupt this pattern and replace it with service from inspired individuals who are 'proud to serve' in an area where they have passion and knowledge.

Let's pick two areas to illustrate this point – high street retail and the hotel and restaurant business.

In fashion retail I'd love to be served by someone who understood fashion and could advise me. More often than not they aren't even familiar with the stock they carry. Does "if we've got it, it'll be out" sound familiar? Then there are the electrical retailers that employ people who know nothing about the goods they're employed to help me buy and the best they are able to do is read from the product cards. I can do that for myself for goodness sake!

Or what about the computer retailers that employ techies who know the industry yet are clueless about how to speak to non-techies in a language we can understand. Or in restaurants when the waiter doesn't even know what the soup of the day is! I'd love just once when I say "I adore fish – what dish can you recommend?" for them to make an enthusiastic recommendation instead of the usual: "Dunno. I haven't tried any of it."

The first pattern to break could be in recruitment. This could start by establishing a potential employee's passion for your product or services. It seems to me the only criteria being applied is if they can speak English and can fill the shifts then they're employed. This will damage your brand reputation and push ever increasing numbers of customers away from the high street and onto the web for online sales, or to the take-away, or the latest celeb cook book for stay-at-home dining.

So, if your staff are working in fashion make sure they know fashion (even if this is simply knowing about your stock). If they're working in cosmetics they must be obsessive about colour trends, face shape, or how to apply that blusher, rather than the sales target set for the next age-reversing foundation. Staff should know their product – be it food, clothes or cosmetics. They must be involved and they must have passion for their subject.

> *"Every thought is a seed. If you plant crab apples, don't count on harvesting Golden Delicious"* Bill Meyer

This can be applied right across the business world. Too many times customers are served by staff less informed than they are. Breaking a customer's reverie or 'pattern interrupt' requires great communication from inspired leaders but a larger part requires enquiring and clued-up members of staff who are curious enough to get the latest information for themselves.

As I have already said, this is not rocket science but obvious, common sense stuff and yet it is rarely applied.

Pattern interrupt principles are often regarded as a soft skills issue so they are avoided simply because they are more difficult to measure. How do you put a key performance indicator against customer perception? How do you track and measure the success of creating long-term trust and confidence? How do you assess passion and enthusiasm? I appreciate this is a challenge yet say in response that focusing exclusively on hard skills leads to short-term thinking.

Romancing the Customer™ is no 'kiss and sell' approach to business. It encourages a smouldering seduction rather than the "wham, bam, thank-you ma'am" business approach. It's official – sexy isn't sex and romancing is no quick romp to get customers to buy, especially at a time when they are all tightening their belts.

Organisations today must understand what customers really want. This approach will help you to understand what customers need, long for, and finally how they judge your competency to deliver these. Getting customers to fall in love with your brand begins with creating confidence and trust. These are the foundations to any lasting relationship, for without them loyalty, love and longevity perish.

How to avoid promiscuity, wanderlust, boredom or an acrimonious break-up is something that leaves many businesses angst-ridden. Yet brand leaders and successful businesses, like great lovers, understand how to avoid this. Their every thought, every action and total commitment is to create moments of bliss by understanding what captivates, creates loyalty and keeps us coming back for more.

CHAPTER TWO

······

Dare to be different

Dare to be different

The habit by so many businesses of focusing, many times with laser-like precision, on areas where they're unable to compete – be this price, choice, convenience, big brand name – results in confusion for employees and cynicism among consumers.

British business today is also suffering from institutionalised imitation, ie a 'me too' mentality.

As markets become ever more saturated, where consumer spend is diminishing and the competition becomes ever more fierce, it would make absolute sense to 'create differential' in order that you stand out from the crowd. To create customer loyalty a continual and sustained strategy of romancing is going to separate the great from the exceptional.

The choice for consumers is now so vast, not just on the high street but also from web-based sales, resulting in an increasing need to create differentiation. Institutionalised imitation goes with the territory for innovative and iconic brands. They expect to be copied and so factor this into their everyday thinking. That's what makes them so captivating.

And this is where many of the casualties in 2009 got it so badly wrong. They created differential, seduced us into falling in love with them, and then rested on their backsides! They committed the cardinal sin in the creation of lasting relationships – they took us for granted. We didn't fall out of love with them, they fell out of love with us. A walk down any high street will illustrate who these retail casualties were.

"It is an immutable law in business that words are words, explanations are explanations, promises are promises but only performance is reality"
Harold Geneen

In relationships it's the equivalent of sitting in front of the TV instead of talking, or relying too much on the socks and pants fairy. In other words, not making an effort, being too busy and then assuming our loved one will remain in love with us. They won't.

You may at this point be asking why bother to create this elusive differential when it seems every time you do the 'me too' element appears, and before you know it your brilliant differential gets eroded.

We bother because daring to be different is the key to brand and business success. Being safe is a very risky strategy so it's perhaps helpful to share some innovative ways for you to create a lasting differential, and one that's totally exclusive to you.

The parallel between memorable romance and memorable business is something I have studied for a number of years (much to the dismay of my parents, amusement of friends and, I would suggest, as part of my dedicated research).

From my relationship history it is clear I'm a serial romantic – I'm always falling madly in love with someone or something. Clearly I am happiest in this state of complete madness – all in the name of professional research of course.

What it has allowed me to do is understand what makes relationships work and what causes them to disintegrate. And this led to thinking about how business can adopt these principles to create brand fidelity.

Let's begin with a question. Do you remember what it was like when you first started to romance someone? When you had those initial stirrings of longing? That first crush? Those delicious sensations you felt for the object of your desire? The obsessive thoughts that were all consuming?

To begin with we're always thinking about them. We search for ways to surprise and delight them. This might be the discovery of an 'our tune' soundtrack, buying cute and amusing things simply because we know they'll just love them, or giving them gifts for no apparent reason.

We want to discover all about their interests, their funny little ways (that strangely become psychotically irritating over time but I digress) and sometimes we even adopt their unique expressions. It can be a damned expensive business too. New outfits (I'm a woman, of course I'll buy new outfits!), gorgeous lingerie, fragrances, meals out… oh the list is endless.

> *"Nothing binds us like a promise kept. Nothing divides us like a promise broken"*
> Mass Mutual

In summary, we want to know everything about them and we often adapt our behaviour to captivate, seduce and get them to see that there isn't anyone out there who can make them feel like we can. We want to make them happy. And we do so consistently.

Just like brand leaders in fact.

Great brands are obsessive about their customers. Their every thought, every action and total commitment is focused upon how to capture their imagination and ultimately their hearts and minds. And what it will take for them to really trust us. They want to know what their customers are looking for. What delights them. What turns them on and what turns them off. What will make them return again and again. What will stop them from looking anywhere else.

Great romance, when done well, is a totally sensory experience. And great business, when done well, is exactly the same. It taps into our emotions rather than our intellect, and is responsible for seducing and getting customers to fall in love with the brand experience. These principles have, and always will, maintain commercially successful brands – irrespective of the service or product being supplied.

One of the first steps to creating a 'dare to be different' approach is to understand first of all who it is you're looking to romance. Who do you want falling in love with your brand? More importantly, who is going to be looking for what you have?

So often I hear businesses say that's impossible to answer as they appeal to everyone, or they're looking for volume, or that they can't afford to be choosy. This approach is flawed and full of danger.

I urge you to be selective – don't throw yourself at everyone. Be courageous, be authentic, and above all else be selective not desperate. Unless you particularly want the promiscuous customer (one night stand, gets what they want never to return) or the unfaithful customer (shops around, uses you until something better comes along), or the high maintenance, demanding customer (nothing you do will ever be good enough), then be selective about who you really want to attract.

Let's run the parallel with dating for a moment.

What? is the first consideration. This often generates such trite, vague and useless responses as "they have to be kind, funny and trustworthy". This is insane. I don't know many people who would deliberately set out to attract an unkind, dull and deeply shifty partner!

The next consideration is: what do I have to offer/who wants what I have? Again this elicits vague responses that do little to create compelling reasons why you're 'the one'. I'm fun (annoying), open-minded (desperate) and outgoing (loud and embarrassing).

We need to consider what it is we do that is truly different, what makes us unique and special, followed swiftly by who we're looking for.

The equivalent in business of 'kind, funny, trustworthy' has to be 'professional, personal service, reliable'… NO! NO! NO! This is the first step down the slippery slope of 'me too brands'. Every other business in your profession will be saying exactly the same thing and it's so predictable. It's also stating the BBO (bleeding bloody obvious) and is largely meaningless drivel.

Your actions, words and the information you provide will communicate far more about your professionalism, your personal service and your competency. Or at least they should. I urge you to replace the usual banality with some thought and consideration for the individual reading it, and for the message it sends out about you.

CHAPTER THREE

......

The power of a good word

The power of a good word

Here is a humorous, and some consider extreme, example of the power of words. I believe it is a sure fire way to illustrate the power of copy and how potent it can be. I have taken my inspiration from the lonely hearts ads found in the dailies (I was looking as part of my research, OK?). These are unedited, real examples for those cynics who think I made it up.

"Go getter seeks romance – attractive, blonde, wants romantic, caring partner. No baggage"

"Indian M, chubby, shaved head, very hairy, likes pubs & eating out"

"Cuddly single Mum seeks M who likes children & nights in"

These are not many words and yet already we've formed a picture of this person (contact details

available upon request). It is no different with the copy
or language we use in our brochures, our websites,
our voicemail, and our direct contact with customers.

What does yours really say about you?
Does it really reflect your brand personality?
How predictable are you being? How focused
on you and not them is it? How much of it is
meaningless puff? How safe is your approach?
How alluring and persuasive is it? Are you trying
to say too much?

Pick a message and then stand proud and tall
(you can impress them later by unfurling your other
amazing talents when appropriate).

If your personality, or that of your business,
is different from the competition because you
have a good sense of humour, you're enthusiastic,
slightly eccentric, deeply knowledgeable, highly
experienced, friendly, approachable, etc then let
this come through in the copy or the language
you use. And don't *tell* me, *show* me.

THE POWER OF A GOOD WORD

An example of brand personality shining through from words would be Innocent. One of their smoothies has a gorgeous way of communicating the need to "shake before use". It says "ingredients may separate" followed by *. Searching around the label for the * announces "but mummy still loves daddy" – cute and very on brand. Asda breweries produce a real ale (one of my passions) called Gentleman Jack and they need to communicate the rather bland requirement about being over 18 to consume the product. This is done wonderfully – "If you're lucky enough to look under 21 we may ask you to prove your age". Spot on!

Telling me how good you are rarely means anything. Use your copy to create a mental picture of what I'm likely to get (which of course is consistent with the service I receive). Ease of understanding, a great experience and clear messages affect our mood and decision processes – especially when it comes to parting with cash, irrespective of the product or service being written about.

Consistency is the vital element to successful brand delivery. Using the right words and tone does take time to craft but it is definitely worth it. Best of all, because it's an area that is unique to you and your business it is not so easily copied by the pesky 'me too' element. This is a powerful commercial advantage that few businesses can ignore.

Once you have the 'who', you will easily be able to create compelling copy by 'talking their language'. Use copy that will appeal to your market as well as communicate 'why you' in a powerful and distinctive style. It will do more to communicate your brand personality and quality than you might imagine. Clarity in communication is the key to successful sales but it must be persuasive to be commercially successful. I urge you to consider using the professional services of a wordsmith or copywriter. This is what they do so they will know how to craft something resembling interesting and jargon free copy, and they'll do a far better job than you ever could. Remember what you're brilliant at and view using the skills of a copywriter as a necessary investment.

THE POWER OF A GOOD WORD

If you do nothing else, hold in mind the following: "It's not about you!" Every single detail or feature you decide to mention must have as its purpose an aim to connect with the person reading it. Customers are all ultimately tuned into the frequency of WIIFM (what's in it for me?) so use this fact to edit and select every point you're thinking of making. If it's there to serve the ego factor (yours not the customer) then it needs to be remodelled to communicate the same message but in a way that describes how your customer can benefit by choosing you. For more about the ego factor, see Chapter 7: It's not about you!

Embrace the dare to be different approach with your copy and see what response you get. From my writing and my personal voicemail alone I have been described as unorthodox, sexy, controversial, distinctive, sublime, knowledgeable, professional, passionate, innovative, enthusiastic, quality, an enigma… Yay! is my first response. Wow! is my next. These are people who have never met me and yet they have a potent image in their mind of who and what I am simply from the words I use.

CHAPTER FOUR

......

The power of a good spoken word

The power of a good spoken word

If we're all tuned into channel WIIFM (what's in it for me) then it makes sense to also communicate verbally in a WIIFM style. Every opportunity needs to be taken to communicate what it is you can do for the customer. This requires effort and a determination to listen, really listen, to the other person. And observe. This will ensure every encounter counts.

I don't have Jedi mind powers and I'm not hypnotising anyone but people often comment on how effortlessly I appear to connect with others. I believe I have been doing this for almost all of my life so it has now become second nature. And it doesn't matter who the person is – the checkout operator, the waiter, the really important client – they all deserve my attention and respect. Admittedly, with different intensities, but each will receive attention and respect.

I make a point of empathising, sharing a joke, saying thank you or just having a bit of a flirt. Sometimes it comes back to bite me on the bottom. Sometimes I'm met with indifference. Other times I get strange looks from people (I have no problem being viewed as the eccentric). This has little to do with being that psychotically irritating person who is perpetually jolly; it's about being polite and having a natural conversation.

> *"Could a greater miracle take place than for us to take a look through each other's eyes for an instant?"*
> Henry David Thoreau

In the pub, the restaurant or the coffee bar it generally gets me pretty good service. At the very least they are friendly towards me. We each have a pleasant encounter.

And I do the same in business. I ask about things they like, things they are happy with, things they are concerned about. And I listen. If they say they are happy with their customer service levels, if they say they are happy that they are doing the right things consistently, and if they say they are not concerned in the slightest about how well they enrich and inspire their customers, then great.

I avoid wasting their time or mine explaining something to them that they wouldn't be interested in and wouldn't be listening to anyway. Also, they would only feel bored or 'sold to' – the inevitable perception when you launch into your services and products without understanding what your customers are concerned about. How awful if someone really fancied what you had to offer only to be bored to death by your talking about something they weren't interested in!

Create the connection and save yourself (and them) an awful lot of heartache and regret.

ESPRESSO YOURSELF

Just take a little time to think about what it is you do and how you could communicate this in a refreshing, professional, cliché-free style. Make sure it is focused on their needs, wants, and desires rather than your agenda.

Go on. Wake people up a little, I dare you!

> *"To make a living is no longer enough. Work also has to make a life"*
> Peter Drucker

CHAPTER FIVE

......

What do people really say?

What do people really say?

This concerns how people talk about their perception of your brand, their experience of your services and their desire to repeat the process time after time. And yet it is also about how accurately they describe your services and products to other people.

Knowing this will safeguard you against spending time, money and energy on creating changes, marketing campaigns or introducing incentives that no-one really cares about. You need to find ways of asking rather than assuming you know what people think, feel and believe about your brand. To illustrate what I mean I'll share an experience I had a few months ago with the aim of helping you to avoid the same frustration and pitfall.

I was part of a networking group consisting of a wide-ranging sector from the local business community. Every week I would present (in lively and witty ways I thought) what it is I do for my clients and why it would be rather marvellous for their contacts to be introduced to me. I did this for months until one morning I received a referral into a large professional federation who were looking for a conference speaker.

> *"O wad some power
> the giftie gie us.
> To see ourslel's
> as others see us!"*
> Robbie Burns

My first thought was: "Yay! Brilliant. Thank you, thank you, thank you!" And then I looked at the email my esteemed associate sent to the federation's director (please hold in mind this was a major federation. Mammoth proportions. The Daddy of conferences. No, I'm not bitter in the slightest).

WHAT DO PEOPLE REALLY SAY?

Apart from the email being riddled with typos (what's wrong with using F7 on the computer?), it began by introducing me as "heading up a local speaking club". This clearly has the same gravitas as President of the Midlands Professional Speakers Association… not! This was promptly followed by "she talks about seduction, or something like that" and ended with "she dresses nicely".

Now I'm not a violent person by nature but the urge to punch this person very, very hard on the nose was overwhelming. However, I chose to inwardly seethe with deadly indignation instead. Remembering the message from my *Zen Approach to Really Irritating Situations*, I was able to choose my response (yep, hitting them is a response).

And what did I learn from this? It's that I'm responsible for how others describe me and my company. I'm responsible for ensuring people use a style and language aligned to my brand. I'm responsible for people representing my company in a way that is accurate and professional. No-one else.

ESPRESSO YOURSELF

The action I decided to take to prevent this ever happening again was easy, didn't involve violence of any kind and now protects what people say to introduce my business. Consider using the same and avoid having to buy a copy of the *Zen Approach to Really Irritating Situations*.

- Create a template for employees and business associates to use when introducing you and your company via email or in any written communication

- Use this same template in a postcard format that can be given to new contacts when you're first introduced

- Get your brand definition and values into every team member's induction (this is not a mission statement, which are on the whole verbose, pointless and deeply boring)

- Establish that a clear understanding has taken place with everyone associated with the brand – this includes suppliers, associates, colleagues, and everyone who is a direct ambassador for what you do and how you do it.

WHAT DO PEOPLE REALLY SAY?

If the people representing your brand haven't been properly briefed and inducted to the company then they will be forced to make things up from the impression they have about you, the little snippets of information they have gathered and finally any experience they have had of your business.

I fell into the 'assume' attitude rather than 'ask' attitude with the experience I have shared. I assumed they would refer to the website. I assumed they would ask me for clarification. I assumed they would have heard what I had been saying. I assumed they understood.

They don't. They won't. They haven't.

CHAPTER SIX

......

Get away from the given!

Get away from the given!

In the same way that inconsistent visual standards undermine your customer's confidence and communicate more than you might have imagined, the taste of your brand is created by the same consistency and virtual red thread. This needs to be running through everything associated with your business. As soon as something breaks this red thread it creates a disconnection in the mind of your customer. It gives them a reason to doubt you. It undermines their confidence.

Consider how your personal presentation, and that of your team and associates, fits with the rest of your brand.

Personally I hate that it matters, and many criticise me as being shallow for even mentioning it but what customers see will determine the perception of your brand, the price they are willing to pay, how much they trust you, how confident they feel and whether they are prepared to recommend and refer your services and products to others.

Hate it or love it, the notion that how you look will be having a direct impact on your success is more prevalent today than ever before.

> *"Seldom do people discern eloquence under a threadbare cloak"* Juvenal

I'm not about to launch into what colours you should be wearing, what styles suit your body shape, or what your choice of pen says about you (unless it's a chewed and bitten one, in which case stop using it). This is more of an appreciation of how important personal image is to your consistent brand identity and the taste perception you create.

You have no doubt heard the stats about how quickly we make our mind up about someone. It takes about 10 seconds to decide whether we like them or trust them, do they fit with our idea, are they fit for the job, etc?

GET AWAY FROM THE GIVEN!

We judge all the time on a personal level and in business customers are even more critical. You have to fit with their expectation otherwise you're going to have to work especially hard to compensate and convince them of your abilities and competency.

This is not to suggest for a moment that everyone in your organisation becomes a clone. I've worked in those companies and it's deeply disturbing. It simply means that if you decide to be a radical non-conformist then prepare for some rejection and unpredictable responses.

For example, I recently presented to an audience on this very issue and during the Q&A a young woman challenged my view (and curiously that of her employer) that as a solicitor she needed to cover her tattoos. Her assertion was that "she was more than her tattoos, she was a great legal mind". Now this is a fair enough point, although I had to explain that for a large part of the population tattoos have a negative association. That for my generation and older, they're taboo, and they certainly weren't what you'd expect to see plastered on the arms of a solicitor. I'm loathed to say it, but tattoos on a woman are considered even more shocking.

On a less extreme level of personal compromise, I recall being invited into the office of the MD while I was an employee of the previously mentioned cloned and deeply disturbing company. This was to have a chat about how I was fitting into the role. During this discussion, I was told: "You do wholesome very well. Clearly you don't need to wear much make-up. However Angi, we don't do wholesome, we do sophisticated. You must remember this is London not Gloucestershire so you must always wear lipstick. Oh, and while we're at it, mind your footwear."

Speechless, I left the office and immediately called a girlfriend for a session of mutual indignation. This friend then offered a wonderful perspective – if all I needed to do to be successful was wear heels and slap on a bit of lippy every hour then it was going to be a breeze.

GET AWAY FROM THE GIVEN!

Suffice to say, several lipsticks and a few pairs of high heels later, I left. I never really let go of the resentment I felt that my competency was being judged in this way.

> *"I try not to break the rules, but merely test their elasticity"*
> Bill Veeck

Rather like the world of romance, they had seduced me, entered into a relationship based on who I was, only to then want to change me when we became 'an item'. I felt betrayed. My contribution and my ability should more than compensate for any absence of lipstick.

But it never would. The image for that company had been carefully crafted, they had worked hard to develop it and everything and everyone needed to maintain this in a seamless, consistent manner, totally reflective of the brand. I was simply at odds with a world that was so specious. Being a rebellious, non-conformist I always felt compelled to flout the lipstick rule. I now value the lesson being taught, as it was about grooming and brand image.

I would say in summary when it's your business you can do as you please and take the consequences but when you're representing an employer you have to fit with their brand image. If the image you have doesn't fit then search around until you're able to find a tattoo friendly law firm or a brand that doesn't care about lipstick and heels.

Meanwhile, get out the long sleeved shirts and slap on the lippy!

CHAPTER SEVEN

......

It's not about you!

It's not about you!

I work with people from a broad range of professions and industries, all of whom have had to study hard to get their professional qualifications. They then use them like a badge of honour or a shield against the world, in the belief that this is all they need to produce in order for customers to fall at their feet.

Many of the letters mean little to a customer and many of the titles they get hung up on matter even less. Who is it all for I wonder? I certainly care more about their ability to connect with me on a personal level than lists of qualifications or where they qualified (think Harold Shipman for goodness sake!).

This is often a professional ego trip and is a total waste of time and energy. As the customer I need to be reassured that you know what I'm looking for, you understand my needs and concerns and you can match these with a perfect solution. This is far more important than professional gobbledy gook.

ESPRESSO YOURSELF

By all means list your qualifications and professional associations, just not at the top of the page or as your main point of difference in conversations or communication.

Pivotal to being the GO TO brand every time is the ability to understand clearly the measures a customer uses to test your competency as a provider of services or products. The customer rarely, if ever, uses the same measure as we do to determine our competency.

Let me offer an example. When describing the services of my accountant I don't recall ever having said: "He's amazing you know, and he's an FCA and is a member of the Institute of Chartered Accountants. Having gained his ACA & AAT qualification with Pocketit in Durham he minimises my exposure and helps me plan robustly." What I'm apt to say is: "My accountant is a great guy, knows his stuff, saves me money and he's really friendly. His office is lovely and I always nick the sweeties from the bowl on reception." (Yes Mark, it's me.)

IT'S NOT ABOUT YOU!

Or there's my optician. Fab guy, knows his stuff, tells me about the health of my eyes, how I can prevent galloping old age turning me blind, we have a good laugh and he explains in a jargon-free manner what changes there has been with contact lens technology and what I could consider using to best meet my needs. Simple.

And yet not. It appears there is much to keep them awake at night, and it centres on what they're allowed to call themselves. It all sounds desperately complicated, with long words I can barely pronounce, let alone spell (something to do with ophthalmologists, optometrists, dispensing opticians, opticians). See, you've lost the will to live already and all for something I, as the customer, couldn't give two hoots about!

My guess is you probably don't care very much either (unless you're an optician, ophthalmic surgeon or other thing beginning with O). Like me, you have assumed that by opening a store that says Optician above the door it's fit for purpose, that the staff can advise me on my eye health and that if they were plumbers they probably wouldn't be working in my local optician.

> *"Years may wrinkle the skin but to give up enthusiasm wrinkles the soul"* Samuel Ullman

I don't know the difference between them, and really it doesn't matter. All that's important is they provide me with the service and the expertise I'm looking for. If they fail to do this then I can reasonably expect to report/sue/prosecute/stalk them.

This is what I mean by professional ego getting in the way of how clients measure competency.

CHAPTER EIGHT

......

Wake me up
or I'll go go

Wake me up or I'll go go

The notion of waking people up, or interrupting the pattern, is a feature that will run through all of the *Romancing the Customer*™ series and it is designed to stir us from our waking slumbers or default coma mode. It is one of the easiest, most effective ways to create brand differential.

For example, if I were to say "roses are red", the likelihood is you would be able to accurately predict what was coming next. In the same way that if I was to start my website with "welcome to same old, same old, we pride ourselves on…", you wouldn't be a million miles from guessing what follows.

> *"Words without actions are the assassins of idealism"*
> Herbert Hoover

ESPRESSO YOURSELF

Or what about the voicemail message that starts with the ubiquitous: "Sorry I'm unable to take you're call at the moment, I'm either..." This is just dull, dull, dull. It is also predictable and leads to boredom. Customers see you as no different to everyone else. They are not engaged and wonder why they should do business with you.

You can create easy stories for customers to share through daring to be different and releasing them from a world of predictability and boredom. They'll love you for it. Certainly they'll remember you for it, and they might even be impressed, if for no other reason than you made them smile or amused them in some way for a few minutes. And be enthusiastic. This alone will create a refreshing change in today's business world. Smile when you record the message. Script it. Change it regularly. Make an effort. It does wake people up and it will elicit a response. Dare to be different because it costs nothing.

CHAPTER NINE

......

Craft a
top 5

Craft a top 5

As you will have already read, throughout the *Romancing the Customer*™ series I advocate thinking a little differently. Part of this is the notion of crafting a top five approach to create relevance and meaning in the mind of your customer as well as powerful connections. The fact that they lead to sales is a given.

You might also like to consider introducing a top five strategy to get to know your team, your associates and your suppliers in a more meaningful way. The fact that this leads to great advocates for you and your brand, lowers attrition and protects your profits is also of huge benefit.

There are simply hundreds of books on opening and closing the sale. Many techniques have been developed encouraging you to identify customers' 'pain' to create additional sales, for getting referrals and for being the number one sales person.

The top five is a different approach to this very subject and may sit more easily with those of you concerned or uncomfortable with the techniques described in these publications. Practice, develop your own top five and accept they need to be flexible.

> *"Nothing encourages creativity like the chance to fall flat on one's face"*
> James D. Finley

Let's begin with how I use these in my personal life and how I have found the process brilliantly illuminating (thanks to Nick Hornby's *High Fidelity* for getting me started on this). An added bonus is the fun and hilarity it creates in the pub. It is nevertheless rather brilliant for helping to build immediate connections (or not as the case may be) simply because they help to bypass much of the fluff and nonsense around many individuals. If you have embraced the 'be selective not desperate' approach already mentioned you will have a clear idea of who it is you're looking for, what they need to be interested in, what you have which matches this and whether you have sufficient common values and philosophies to sustain a mutually beneficial relationship.

Some of my personal top fives centre around what it is the other person needs to be interested in to 'float my boat' so I tend to focus on the areas which I'm deeply passionate about.

I begin by asking what are their top five films, books, sound tracks, indulgences, foods, most unattractive habits, favourite ways to waste time, things that create bliss for them, or things that drive them mad.

"To be nobody but yourself in a world which is doing its best night & day to make you like everybody else means to fight the hardest battle any human being can fight. Never stop fighting"

EE Cumming

If I'm unfamiliar with their choices I ask for more details to get a better understanding. I also love it when the top fives match. Rather like great interview questions, a top five approach cuts through things to discover the real person. In many ways I have found it creates a shortcut to stop me from wasting time or creating future heartbreak.

Applying it to business can offer the same benefits.

In the world of business using a top five approach gets to the nub of the other person's issues very quickly. It means you have to really listen. It means the other person is the centre of the conversation. And it means you can truly demonstrate how much you care. It is a brilliant way to help you determine whether you have the solution they are looking for. More importantly it can help you to understand the most effective way of communicating this solution or what I call the flirting and showing off stage (more of this later).

CRAFT A TOP 5

Here are some top five suggestions for you to use in business:

- Things they're looking for from a trainer/accountant/solicitor/consultant/skincare company

- Things that disappoint them with their current provider (if this is the first time for them using your products or services then ask what their top five fears are)

- Concerns they have in their business

- Benefits of addressing these concerns

- Best outcomes

- Best measures

- Key challenges

In fact it can be anything which will help to illuminate their dreams, hopes, desires and which will also help to focus them on life with you in it. Design an approach that feels comfortable for you and helps to address the top five. Avoid asking them in the style of a pilot's checklist, however. Develop a way of incorporating them into a natural conversation and practice. I promise it is great fun and very powerful for creating that elusive brand fidelity.

Flirting and showing off

I have been described as a dreadful flirt (although personally I think I'm pretty good at it). I flirt all the time. With everyone. My friends, my family, my business associates, complete strangers, on stage, in business meetings, in the supermarket, in restaurants, everywhere. It doesn't get me arrested, molested or accosted by strange individuals (well, sometimes maybe). It does get me great service, wonderful friendships, great business and a fabulous reputation for being inspiring, provocative and interesting. It supports what I was taught as a child – every encounter counts. You never know when you're creating a memory. So what memory do you create with your encounters?

CRAFT A TOP 5

And what greater evidence is there of a total show off than someone crazy enough to stand up on stage and speak for a living? It's when you show off and flirt in the right measures that you create delightful memories and inspiration for those around you. It becomes totally uplifting, charming, sublime and enriching, or at least it should.

Flirting

It has been suggested I need to explain what flirting means in the wonderful world of women and how this may differ for men. It is not my aim to be sexist here and I apologise for any offence given. It is simply a fact of life. Men and women interpret things differently, so I offer the following as a definition of what I mean.

Flirting is no more than demonstrating how well you're listening and/or paying attention to the other person. You find ways to say and do pleasant things or pay compliments for no other reason than because you can. The other person feels amazing and you feel amazing. This must, must, must be packed with integrity, sincerity and authenticity. It has no agenda other than to create a connection. "It is attention without intention", as Max O'Rell says. It's simply being deeply interested in the other person and what it is they need/are interested in/want to know more about. It's about being fully 'in the moment' irrespective of whether this is at work, in the supermarket or in a restaurant.

> "Never underestimate the power of passion" Eve Sawyer

Showing off

Showing off is simply listening out for the need/interest/want to know more about element of the conversation. When you show off it is simply to demonstrate how you've helped others with this in the past. It is never about being the big I am or bragging, it is about self-effacing modesty to show you have heard them, you're familiar with what they're talking about and you have experience which may interest them. Keep showing off to a minimum and always link it back to the other person.

CRAFT A TOP 5

Both flirting and showing off in a business context, when done spontaneously, with oodles of natural charm and genuineness demonstrate your professional confidence – in your abilities and intentions as well as in their best interests.

It means you don't necessarily have the best 'stuff' or are the cheapest or the biggest. What it does mean is that you understand what they want and need and how they see things working.

And confidence is massively sexy (sexy doesn't mean sex, it means being irresistible). Professional and personal confidence makes you glow and it attracts attention. It reinforces your natural strengths and avoids you falling into the trap of the 'me too' brigade. It is also tremendous fun, which is something sadly lacking in most areas of business.

When flirting and showing off is done with genuine charm it is a clear sign that you feel comfortable. There is no awkwardness. And if you feel confident and comfortable chances are your customer will feel the same. Confidence breeds confidence.

ESPRESSO YOURSELF

Finally, it means you and your brand become totally persuasive and the experience is instantly repeatable.

The reasons for *Romancing the Customer*™ are no different to the world of relationships. Once you've captured their heart, you've captured the person. And they've fallen in love with you. You want to keep them. You don't want their eyes to wander and you certainly don't want them to try another brand.

> *"People are like stained-glass windows. They sparkle and shine when the sun is out, but when darkness sets in their true beauty is revealed only if there is light from within"*
> Elizabeth Kübler-Ross

CHAPTER TEN

......

Conclusion

Conclusion

Espresso Yourself is the beginning of shifting away from corporate thinking and moving the focus firmly back where it belongs – on the customer.

As I said in the introduction, now more than ever, there must be a renaissance in exceptional service, inspired expertise, creative thinking and innovation by businesses. The brands and organisations that thrive and prosper in good and bad times are those who think differently and consequently behave differently.

There needs to be an understanding and commitment by businesses to implement a strategy of continued effort in the desire to always be 'the one'. Where once unenthusiastic service, indifferent, lazy business professionals and ambivalence towards customers was tolerated, it has rapidly become replaced by an expectation that they're going to be inspired and educated by individuals fired by passion and knowledge.

ESPRESSO YOURSELF

That customers' needs, wants and wishes are going to be exceeded, because if they're not, they will simply move on to someone who will fulfil these.

For brands to be profitable and relevant, they have to embrace the notion of *Romancing the Customer*™ to create the much sought after loyalty, delight and longevity of relationships with their customers. This is the only way to avoid the pitfalls of promiscuity, boredom and indifference.

> *"You know you're in love when you don't want to fall asleep because the reality is finally better than your dreams"* Dr Seuss

Wake people up. Dare to be different. Stir the passions. Inspire. Bring absolute pleasure. Become obsessive. Get involved.

Above all else, romance!

About the author

About the author

Angi's retail pedigree is as diverse as it is distinguished – primarily with global household brands such as the Body Shop International, IKEA, Gap and M&S and finally with ESPA at Harvey Nichols and Liberty in London.

She has worked as a consultant with anything from cars, motorbikes, spectacles, skincare and wine merchants through to national charity organisations.

Within her retail career Angi gained knowledge and experience through successful senior management positions in all aspects that this multi-disciplined profession demands – operations, marketing, shop floor, manufacturing and finally retail merchandising.

Developing and refining her understanding from some of the best retailers, Angi quickly established herself as a natural retailer who loved nothing better than the thrill of seeing customers buy. She also recognised her innate capacity to lead and inspire individuals to achieve team and personal goals.

These are Angi's natural passions – retail and leadership – something she puts down to being 'proud to serve'. She discovered during her 20-year retail career that this requires dedication, courage, humility and commitment – some qualities she had in abundance, others she needed to discover through early mistakes.

With an instinctive feel for what works, what looks right and what will surprise and delight the customer, she is rapidly becoming recognised as one of the most innovative retail specialists. Her approach is contemporary, highly relevant and totally fresh, and her overriding priority is to maintain a laser-like focus on the commercial gains open to the retailer.

Based in the historic jewellery quarter in Birmingham, she works with businesses across the UK and internationally.

What people say about Angi Egan

"Angi is a real joy to work with. She gets to the heart of customer feelings and how to practically reinforce their relationship with your services and brand. She did a great job visually revamping our reception and front office area, creating just the right atmosphere for our services for older people."
Michael Vincent, Chief Executive, Age Concern Coventry

"Angi makes you think. Makes you change. Makes you money."
Andy Clark, Founder and CEO of Speakers Academy

"Angi has an uncanny knack of finding all those winning ways and making them into compelling, easy-to-follow success strategies. She makes you wonder why they never seemed so obvious before she worked her magic!"
Gilbert Vasey, SpecSavers, Crystal Peaks, Sheffield

"Angi has a unique gift for making the difficult seem simple. Her theories and principles make sense and are accessible for all, from the experienced businessman through to the enthusiastic start up. From personal experience, I know that her messages make an instant and positive difference."
David Hyner, Managing Director, Stretch Development Ltd and professional speaker

"If there is one business book you should read this year it's this one! In these times, you need her informed insights into customer seduction more than ever."
Roger Harrop, President of the Professional Speakers Association

Praise for the Angi's first book in the
Romancing the Customer™ series – Initial Lust.
The Key to Visual Communication & Brand Marketing

"Finally, a narrative which cuts through generational gaps to communicate a traditional message in a way that means even the most cynical employee understands about service."
Jane Barnett, National Education Manager, Kérastase, Paris

"Should have a public warning attached – I laughed out loud with the cheeky style of writing but was impressed with the insights and approaches."
Bernard Molloy, FCILT FBICs, Managing Director,
HOPPECKE Industrial Batteries Ltd

"My initial lust soon became "love". This is a great read and Angi Egan has got the balance just right. In a sense this book taught me what I already know... but I'm not currently doing! It has great content, is written with great style and exceeded my expectations at every stage."
Phil Jesson, Director of Speaker Development,
The Academy for Chief Executives

"Never more than now, in these financially troubled times, do "people buy from people". However, it wasn't until I read Initial Lust by Angi Egan that I truly understood the importance of creating the relationship. Features and benefits fall second to this approach."
Malcolm Gibbs, Q&A Management Services

Coming soon…

THE BARRY WHITE EFFECT – YEH BABY!

The Power of Auditory Messages for Your Brand

. . . .

This book looks at everything concerned with the auditory messages surrounding a brand, from background music to voicemails, dialogue with teams and suppliers through to the power of the spoken word to inspire, create trust, reinforce authority and elevate quality.

The spoken word also has huge significance in how we engage and connect with different generations. Communication with multi-generational workforces must be relevant and attractive in order to connect. Failure to do so will mean the rapid demise of consumer loyalty and business profits.

We currently have a generation who believe sales is about standing and taking the money, albeit in a gorgeous and polite way. They have neither the skills nor the vocabulary for what we now demand of them. The book calls for business professionals to take responsibility to provide these skills in a manner that is fun, engaging and relevant, otherwise the message will never stick. The metaphor of the book is romance and is one different generations just 'get'.

The opposite to love is not hate but indifference – and this is what businesses must concern themselves with in order to have relevance and success. This begins with engaging the teams we employ.